T0197580

HELLO MY NAME IS TIFF

A Little Dog's Life Story

AUTHOR **ROBERT J. TURNER III,M.D.,FACS**

ILLUSTRATED BY **JOHN H. SMITH,M.D.,FACS**

Print information available on the last page

Rev. date: 06/14/2019

To order additional copies of this book, contact:
Xlibris
1-888-795-4274
www.Xlibris.com
Orders@Xlibris.com

To: Jamie, Ford, Turner, Anna Caroline, Eliza, India, Estella, Lillie, and grandchildren everywhere

You think dogs will not be in heaven? I tell you, they will be there long before any of us.

ROBERT LOUIS STEVENSON

He is your friend, your partner, your defender, your dog. You are his life, his love, his leader. He will be yours, faithful and true, to the last beat of his heart. You owe it to him to be worthy of such devotion.

ANONYMOUS

A dog has the soul of a philosopher.

PLATO

PREFACE

Our family has had dogs ever since my wife and I married and had our fourth child. We have had a total of six children, but I can't begin to count the number of dogs that we have had. They were an integral part of our family. Tiffany, or Tiff as the name was lovingly shortened to, was our *empty nest* dog. Our second daughter accused us of caring more about Tiff than we did about our grandkids. That was not true, of course, but we did learn to love Tiff more than any other dog that we had ever had. It is hard to explain, but she was just something special, as you will see from reading *her story*.

I got the idea for writing this children's book just after Tiff's death in 1999. I retired from almost 50 years of practicing surgery in 2002. I knew I didn't want to just play golf, so I embarked upon a second career of writing and art. The latter has been an on again, off again life long hobby. This book is the first, and hopefully not the only product, of my new career.

I purposefully did not designate an age reference for the book because I am constantly amazed at the reading capabilities of my grandchildren and therefore thought it might stimulate some dictionary work if a reader is puzzled by an unfamiliar word.

ILLUSTRATIONS FOR HELLO MY NAME IS TIFF

1. Kennel with small and adult dogs.
2. Tiff in a basket with bow.
3. Lion and Lhasa side by side.
4. Tiff scratching on sliding glass door
5. Tiff walking on a leash—lower legs of adult
6. Tiff sitting looking at foundation of town house
7. Tiff on a bed
8. Moving van with Tiff barking at it
9. Tiff with head out of car window
10. Tiff sticking nose through wrought iron railing
11. Tiff sitting by box of dog toys.
12. Tiff going under left side of large wrought iron gate
13. Tiff standing beside luggage with her tail drooping
14. Tiff sticking her head out of a duffel bag
15. Tiff in a carry on pet cage beside an airplane
16. Adult holding Tiff in arms and Jack Russel Terrier biting her rear
17. Tiff barking at a large dog(mastiff)
18. Tiff struggling in a swimming pool
19. Tiff with a small buff colored Lhasa barking at her
20. Tiff in front of Pearly Gates
21. Tiff lying beside a stream of water
22. Head stone with small grave
23. Tiff looking at large palatial structure
24. Tiff standing on a cloud and looking down at the earth

IN THE BEGINNING

Have you ever had a large red bow tied around your neck and then been placed in a red basket like you were an assortment of Valentine candy? Well, that embarrassment happened to me the first time I met Puddin. No that is not a desert or something to eat; It is a real person's name, one of my new human parents. I can still close my eyes and in my mind see her walking towards my kennel, accompanied by the owner, then bending over the fence and asking "Is the little black and white bundle of fur a female?" The owner replied,"Yes; Isn't she adorable?

My husband and I always thought she looked like a little Panda." Puddin picked me up and cuddled the side of her face to mine and it was mutual love at first sight and touch. "I've got to have her." Puddin said. The owner replied "Fine, I'll make all of the arrangements and get the papers to you later". Then Puddin took me in her arms and we went out to one of those whizzing machines which would occasionally come into the kennel's driveway. She opened the door and proceeded to decorate my neck with a large red bow ribbon. Then she put me in the basket as I previously mentioned. I thought, what is this? What have I gotten into? Am I going to be sold in a pet store or raffled at a charity event. Later I found out that I was a Valentine present for her husband and my human father, Bobby.

Allow me to digress a moment and bring you up to date on my background. I was born in a kennel in Burleson, Texas which is a small community south of Fort Worth, Texas, where Puddin and Bobby lived. My real mother told me that my four siblings and I were Lhasa Apsos, just like all of the other dogs in the kennel. She also told us we were from Tibet, originally, and were bred by the Tibetan Monks to be the guard dogs of their palaces. The monks thought we were so smart we could have been re-incarnated monks.

My memory is not clear on the subject of my name. I don't believe the kennel owners named me or my siblings. My name was not really Tiff. Puddin and Bobby named me Tiffany and over the course of my years it was lovingly shortened to Tiff; I guessed it was like a nickname.

My real parents told me about the Lhasa's ability to tell whether a person was a friend or a stranger. My real parents also told me in Tibet we were called Apso Seng Kye which meant barking sentinel lion dog. I guess we do look somewhat like a miniature lion, now that I think about it.

EL CAMPO

After I left the Burleson kennel and my biological parents, Puddin took me to a house on El Campo Street, on the west side of Fort Worth, Texas. I thought this was it; this duplex was my new home, but later I realized that house just provided a temporary home while Puddin and Bobby built the town house of their dreams, located several blocks away in what they called a gated community. I learned all this from listening to them talk. People don't realize dogs listen, think, and even dream. It seemed I was sort of a compromise and what my human parents termed a town house dog. In their old house, which comprised six bedrooms, the family had Golden Retrievers as pets. I didn't know one breed from another but I knew I was a Lhasa Apso. Usually, I just said I saw a large dog or a small one. Some were mean and some were nice and liked to play. From what they said a Golden Retriever must have been too large for a town house and my size worked better. Whatever they wanted; I just welcomed the opportunity to have been there and have been part of their life.

My human parents heaped kindness and attention on me. Puddin taught me to go to the bathroom outside and to not mess inside the house. They did not allow me to go out thefront door unless they attached one of those straps called a leash to my collar. The restriction of mobility made me feel imprisoned but I gradually realized it was for my own safety since my kenneled life had not allowed me to realize the dangers caused by the big loud cars whizzing by all the time. I heard Puddin and Bobby talking about crazy people driving cars, and that was when I learned what you called those whizzers. There was a little side door and I learned if I sat in front of it and barked or scratched it with my paw someone suddenly appeared and opened the door. I likened it to rubbing and uncorking a bottle washed up on the beach and then having a Genie pop out and grant me my wish. I hoped it would never stop-It didn't.

After I grew larger, I went on walks with Puddin and Bobby-on a leash of course.

Everyday Puddin and I walked to the town house under construction. This house was located in a large tree covered area enclosed by a high fence and a large iron gate. I learned many new things. I even noticed the house changing each day. It was like something magical happened each night and when we returned the next day it was different. The first time I saw the house it rested on long red metal beams which were the major part of the foundation and from there it gradually enlarged to a magnificent structure called a Town House.

You wonder how a dog, like me, knew all the technical terms-well I heard my human parents talking about them. I enjoyed seeing changes in the house each day and I guessed that was why we walked over to Highland Park so often. Occasionally I heard Puddin fussing at the workers or the contractor if she thought they were progressing at an unacceptably slow pace.

I amazed Puddin and Bobby with my ability to distinguish sounds and odors. I could differentiate an unfamiliar sound or smell from those previously identified as being associated with a friend or family member. Lhasas just did that because of their breeding. If you remember, I told earlier in my story that my biological parents informed me and my siblings about this power that Lhasas had. It was no big deal, but my human parents thought it incredible. They knew I accomplished it but they couldn't determine how. I wished I had the ability to let them know, but I wasn't that good and besides I really didn't know myself; I just did it, like I was looking into a large crystal ball and determining friend or foe.

All three of us, Puddin, Bobby, and I, slept in a bedroom on the second floor of the El Campo house. At first I had a little bed of my own at the foot of their bed.

Their bed looked so big and "comfy", I thought I would try sleeping there also-if they didn't mind. They were surprised to see a small dog like me jump high enough to get on their bed, so they let me stay. I convinced myself that they liked my company. I slept there ever since.

I loved it when Puddin and Bobby's children visited the house. It was especially fun when they brought their little kids. I tried to play with them as carefully as I could, but they were small and even I knocked them down. I didn't mean to, but their parents thought I played too rough. Later as I got older and more mature, I calmed my relationships with them and we got along much better. I always wanted to be the center of attention and be "on stage" at all times. I did not understand that perhaps the visitors were not coming to see me.

Almost a year had passed since I left the Burleson kennel. I barely remembered my biological parents and siblings, but I knew that I had grown to about their same size and probably would not grow any larger. That was fine with me. I was a town house dog and happy to be considered one.

I saw the construction workers had nearly completed the house in Highland Park (Puddin called it that). The big beautiful house had many neat and cool places to lie down and take little naps. That's what dogs liked to do when they were not running and playing and I was no exception.

HIGHLAND PARK

Finally the day came. A big truck arrived at the little house on El Campo and strange men started moving all of the furniture out of the duplex. At first I didn't understand; Were they trying to rob us, what was going on? I performed my guard thing by barking my head off at the intruders while acting like an attack dog, but for some reason they ignored me. At last I understood what they were doing so I calmed down-we were moving.

At the end of the day we got in the car and drove to the new house. That wasn't the first time I had been in one of those things which whizzed up and down the street. I liked riding in them. I stuck my nose out of the window and felt the rush of cool air on my face; I thought it great, so refreshing, as if you were lying under a shade tree on the cool green grass and feeling a gentle breeze tickle your body, especially your nose.

Tall ceilings and floors made of wood with slabs of stone, intermingled with the polished oak, made the house roomy and absolutely beautiful. The cool stone and wood floors felt so good to my stomach when I stretched out on them; I thought I had my own air conditioner and in Fort Worth that was important. I heard Puddin and Bobby call the stone slabs marble. Three porches provided roaming room for me. It was not like going out into a yard because they had a tile covering rather than grass. Two of the porches in the back of the house extended over a cliff and the first time I stuck nose through the wrought iron railing I thought I was going to fall.

From the back porches, I looked over the beautiful Trinity River valley and observed tall green trees and interesting buildings. At night the same scene sparkled with thousands of lights and made you think you were looking at a distant large city.

I had the run of the house. I went everywhere and climbed on all of the furniture that I could reach. I jumped on the bench at the foot of the bed and then onto the bed itself, without any help. Later in my life they had to pick me up and put me on the bed; my human parents spoiled me so-at least that's what everybody said.

I tried to be a good dog and thought I accomplished that status. I knew because Puddin and Bobby told me so-all the time. I had some bad habits-everybody did. One habit drove Bobby crazy. After I ate, I couldn't stand to have food or grease on my facial hair, so I wiped my face on the couch in the living room or on the wall. I didn't know it left a greasy mark but I didn't have a napkin, so what else could I do. He would go berserk when he saw me doing it. He never hit me with his hand, but he used that old folded paper trick. I thought somewhere they had read that the paper made a loud noise when used to discipline pets, rather than hurting them. It wasn't painful, but it was humiliating or should I have said caniliating.

Times were good. I had my own toy box, my own food and water bowl in the kitchen and on the back porch next to the bedroom.

I barely remembered my real parents, but I still periodically thought about my litter mates. I dreamed about them and wondered if they had found the good life like I had.

My favorite time of the day was late afternoon. Puddin called it the cocktail hour. It didn't happen every day, but often her friends came over for refreshments and they gave me doggie treats. I really liked one friend named Janice. I liked her because she obviously enjoyed me and always gave me little tid—bits. She talked about her dogs and how much she adored them. I could tell she was a special person and one of Puddin's best friends.

I relished the one on one visits, but I didn't enjoy the parties. There were so many people; I always feared someone would step on me. That trauma happened several times and I loudly and forcibly yelped. This always attracted Puddin's attention. She was so kind to me. She picked me up after it happened and made sure I had not been injured. No, my reaction was not just for attention-it really hurt. Although I must admit my pain threshold was low. Most of the time, I left and went off by myself when I thought the party-goers ignored me and removed me from center stage. I then sulked and waited in some cool secluded part of the house for the party to end and have my life return to normal.

At night when I needed to go to the bathroom, I jumped down from the bed and went to the front door and barked one time. This bark differed from the one directed at intruders or strangers. That barking was frantic, hysterical, and continuous. Sometimes Bobby awakened when I jumped down, but if not, the one bark always stimulated him to go to the door and let me go out; then he always left it ajar so I could come back in by myself.

I shimmied under the wrought iron front gate on the left side. I don't know why I always went out and in on that side—both sides were the same. Since a steel fence and large gate enclosed the whole residential complex, there were none of those whizzing cars to worry about. When I came back to bed he closed the front door. What more could a little dog ask?

During the early years at Highland Park, when I was young and frisky, we went for walks on the roads which meandered through-out the fenced and landscaped complex. I liked that because I didn't have to wear one of those leashes as I did when we walked on the streets outside of the gates. I guess you could say I was finicky or prissy and leashes were also part of that attitude. I wouldn't even step in a puddle of water and rain, what my human parents called water that fell out of the sky, made that a real problem. I hated getting wet because I disliked someone drying me before I went into the house. I disapproved of people messing with me. Can you imagine Puddin and Bobby's children thought me spoiled? That was not being spoiled, it was just likes and dislikes.

Talking about being messed with, I really hated going to the groomer and my doctor, the veterinarian. The groomer washed you, trimmed your hair, and fussed with you big time. Some of them were gentle and kind and others were rough and inconsiderate. I think Puddin could tell which ones mistreated me because I trembled and shook when we got close to their place of business. I sensed familiar locations when we rode in the whizzer and this always amazed her. I seemed to possess a built in navigational system; but, like telling friend from foe, I didn't know how I did it. My doctor was considerate and compassionate and I knew he wasn't trying to hurt me; but those things he did, looking, poking, and manipulating, all hurt real bad. I couldn't stand pain.

I remembered Puddin and Bobby talking about taking me to the doctor for him to surgically fix me so I couldn't have babies. I didn't care. I had no great desire to be a mother. After we went to the doctor's office, I remembered lying on a big table with a bright light shining in my eyes. When I awakened, my stomach hurt so bad I could barely walk. It felt like someone prodding me with a red hot poker. Puddin took me home and made a nice little bed on the floor with water and food close by. I needed something more comfortable so I managed to crawl up on the big bed when she wasn't looking and I stayed there for three days, since it took that length of time for the pain to go away. I didn't care how much they talked about me being a big baby, or the other things they said-It really hurt.

I was extremely perceptive. I sensed when my human parents were going to leave the house for an extended period of time. They packed their clothes in things which looked like big brown boxes with handles on them. I became sad and moped around, letting them know how I felt. Puddin could tell when I was depressed-I let my tail droop. Lhasas carried their tail proudly, in a little curl, over their back-unless they were unhappy or sad. Sometimes Puddin and Bobby allowed me to go on trips with them. I could always tell when they desired my company. Puddin gathered my bowls, some toys, and that infernal collar and leash and put them in the whizzer. I was overjoyed. I was going too-what fun.

TRIPS

We went on some neat trips. I liked it best when we traveled to cooler places. It really got hot in Fort Worth and Lhasas came from mountainous Tibet where it was frigid, with lots of snow and ice. I did not approve of snow and ice, but I liked colder weather. Tibet's cold weather generated our heavy fur coat. I understand some Lhasa owners cut their dog's hair in the summer but Puddin refused to even think about it. She said she remembered, when she was a little girl, a collie her family owned. They cut her long beautiful hair for medical reasons and the dog was so ashamed that she hid under the bed. I was delighted she felt that way since I thought I would have acted like the Collie did.

One summer Puddin put me in the whizzer and we went on a long trip to a place which I thought was called Maine. One of her daughters, and a lady friend, went along also.

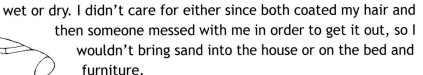

We spent the night in motels as we traveled and sometimes they had to hide me in a bag before we went into the room. I guessed those places didn't like little dogs.

I thought Maine was cool, both in my mind and in the temperature. I remembered we went to a place where you could see water stretching all the way to the horizon. A strip of land which they called the beach paralleled the water and that portion of the shore caused problems for me. The beach consisted of sand which could be wet or dry. I didn't care for either since both coated my hair and then someone messed with me in order to get it out, so I wouldn't bring sand into the house or on the bed and furniture.

The return trip from Maine caused most of the difficulty associated with the vacation. One time Puddin put me in a little cage and we boarded a big bird looking thing which she called an airplane. The next thing I knew we were home. Not bad—except for the cage.

At least it surpassed the time her son drove me home in her whizzer. His name was Kenneth. He took a week to drive home and we were always stopping at weird places. He left me in the whizzer while we stopped and he took care of his business. I did not enjoy being alone, especially in strange places. I didn't have a bath for two weeks. Even I welcomed the groomer in Fort Worth

I especially liked Santa Fe. The weather was so cool and crisp and we stayed in a big neat home that belonged to friends of my human parents. Unfortunately they had two large dogs. The younger one always wanted to play but the older one just ignored me. I didn't mind that. On one occasion we went on a picnic at a park, off the ski mountain road. I ran through the tall grass to my heart's content; it exhilarated me and made me euphoric, as if I was flying by myself. Then along came a mean dog that belonged to one of the guests and he started chasing me. He was about my size but even I couldn't stare him down or bluff him. Puddin yanked me into her arms and the thing jumped up and bit hair out of my bottom. He scared me to death, but mostly the scene embarrassed me. He could have really hurt me. I heard them say, he was a Jack Russell Terrier-whatever that was. I told you I didn't know one breed from another.

Speaking of dog size, one time we went on a long trip to a place called Steamboat Springs, Colorado. It was so-so cool, both in temperature and in experiences. We visited some friends who had a huge dog-I mean really big. I believed they called him a Mastiff. Do you know I actually scared that big dog? I couldn't believe little Tiff capable of such a feat. If I growled at him for fun, he ran away. I was glad he didn't try and see if he could get the best of me. I just bluffed and we got along fine.

That was really a neat trip. I liked Colorado. The only bad thing was it was so far away and, just like Maine, it took so long to drive there and back. I liked those big things which looked like a bird, even if I had to ride in a cage.

THE LATER YEARS

Those are nice words for old age. I gradually lost my sight in one eye. I could see light but it seemed like I was looking through a piece of paper that blurred everything. I heard my human parents say a cataract caused the vision loss. They talked about having it removed but they didn't think it bothered me enough, since it only affected one eye. As the years went by I started having difficulty seeing out of the other eye. Then the strangest thing happened; I lost my usual acute sense of hearing. All of those problems occurred over a period of a year. I hated old age and its associated infirmities. I couldn't jump high enough to get on the bed. My hips hurt and I noticed that all I wanted to do was sleep. Sometimes I perked up, especially when the weather cooled but mostly I just wanted to lie on one of those marble slabs and doze. I had many other health problems but I won't bother you with the details. I always heard Puddin tell people how she despised hearing someone bore you by discussing their ailments. It was a fact, like it or not, I was getting old and I couldn't adjust to it or do anything about it. I was fifteen and that's equivalent to 105 human years, but as you can tell from my story, I had a good life. I had nothing to complain about; except I puzzled about what would be next. Sometimes I thought about my litter mates and wondered if they were still alive or not and, if they were alive, did they despise old age as much as I. I knew that my biological parents must not still be alive. Oh well I couldn't do anything about it anyway.

Then one day it happened again. Some men came into our Highland Park home and started moving the furniture out of the house. I did my Lhasa routine, of course. Puddin became upset because I barked so ferociously. I thought, oh no, not again; we couldn't be leaving this big beautiful house which I loved so much, but it was true. At the end of the day we got into the whizzer and went to a strange house, close to Highland Park. The new house occupied a lot on a very busy street corner, and it seemed to have a large fenced backyard. The new house and large yard confused and alarmed me. The interior of the house smelled like those furry things which people called cats. I could still smell good. At least I had one acutely functioning sense left. I couldn't find my way around the new house and I bumped into things because I could barely see. I sensed my human parents were worried about me because of my inability to cope with my new surroundings. Finally I found the one familiar place which made me comfortable, Puddin's clothes-closet. I spent a lot of time in her closet at the Highland Park house. I could still smell and I loved being around her familiar odor. It gave me a warm furry feeling and a sense of security.

Puddin brought me to the kitchen at mealtime and put me outside afterwards so I could go to the bathroom. I could barely walk since my joints hurt so bad. Sometimes, she noticed my

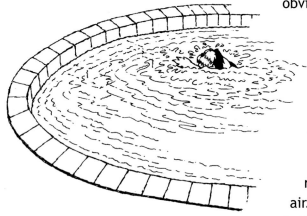

obvious pain and gave me a little pill to help relieve it. Several times when I went outside I fell into a large puddle of water which I found out later was called a swimming pool. I barked frantically and fortunately someone's hand pulled me out.

I never tried to swim before and I didn't want to learn how. Puddin dried me with a towel and she even used one of those blow-dryers to get me warm and dry. They reminded me of a machine which blew dry desert air. I knew because some of the groomers used them. I still hated being messed with but it was better than being cold and wet. My reaction and the falling event embarrassed me. I, who never stepped in water, fell into a large swimming pool. I couldn't see it even if it was large. After the bad pool experiences, they never left me alone when I went outside.

We had been in the house on Byers several months, when the most distressing thing happened. Puddin brought a small frisky dog to the house. I could barely hear but I think I heard them say it was a Lhasa like me except it was buff colored rather than black and white.

The thing wanted to play all the time. I couldn't see it but suddenly I felt it nipping at me. The worst trick it had consisted of slamming its body sideways into me and knocking me down. I was an old lady. She should have been more respectful, but then I remembered being young and frisky once and probably would have done the same thing.

I detected that Puddin and Bobby were concerned about my health and I guessed they wondered if I could be helped. Puddin took me back to my doctor to determine if he could do anything to make me more comfortable. He was kind and gentle but as I told you I hated being messed with. Things were a little better for awhile after that office visit but then inevitably I became worse. I could hardly stand and just walking caused extreme pain and difficulty.

One day Puddin put me in the whizzer and we went to the doctor's office. I couldn't see but I still had an amazing sense of direction and knowledge of my location at all times. I started trembling and doing my usual act, hoping she would feel sorry for me and turn around but, as always, it didn't work. Puddin picked me up and carried me into the office. I noticed she was crying-I mean really sobbing. I had never known her to do that before. She gave me to my kind doctor and he gently put me down on the table. Suddenly I saw a bright light as if it was far off in the distance or at the end of a tunnel. Then it started getting dimmer and dimmer until it finally went out.

HEAVEN

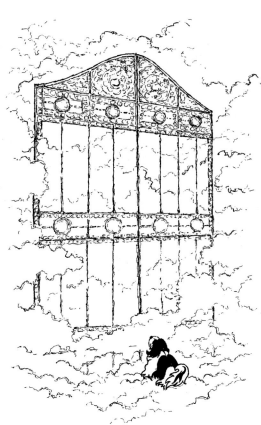

The next thing I knew I was standing in front of a huge white shiny gate made of large round gleaming balls. They looked like a pearl necklace I had seen Puddin wear-just much larger.

Clouds were all around and I was even standing on one. Then suddenly this tall old man with white hair, a long white beard, and holding a large stick appeared in the opening of the gate. In addition, it looked like wings were growing out of his back. I couldn't help it; I gave one of my friendly barks and said,"Hello, my name is Tiff." He replied in a booming voice,"Come on in Tiffany, we have been expecting you in Heaven." "Is this really Heaven?" I asked," I didn't know little dogs were allowed there," I added. "Only special little dogs get to come here and you are certainly one," he answered.

Heaven is everything I ever dreamed about and more. I don't have to worry about my human parents putting out food and water; It's there all the time, as much as you want. The angels distribute the food and treats, which are tasty and completely unlike any I had on earth; I guess they have their own bakery in Heaven. The treats are like cookies and biscuits. They are all shapes and sizes. Some even look like various animals. The angels come around all the time and keep the bowls filled with the treats so I don't have to wait for the cocktail hour as I did on earth. I don't have to worry about someone opening the doors for me to get out or in-they are always open. There are no whizzers running around so there is no danger of getting hurt. It's Heaven. There are rolling fields covered with lush green grass which reminded me of those meadows in Santa Fe. You can run through the grass and over the gently sloping countryside to your heart's content. Beautiful lakes and peaceful streams adorn the landscape and entice you to wade or swim in them. I'm not a swimmer but I love to lie beside them and stare into the shimmering water. It's so peaceful-It's heaven.

There are no masters up here, just God, his Son, angels, and St.Peter-of course. Those are in addition to the fortunate inhabitants. St. Peter seems to organize most of the functions and schedules. You just do what you want and fend for yourself. The human and animal angels are all friendly. Oh yes, there are animal angels. Some have wings and some are just clad in long white robes like everybody else. I understand those who don't have wings are waiting for them so they can be guardian angels.

The pets which are here are all nice and friendly. That is why they are here. There are all sorts-dogs, cats, horses, gerbils, iguanas, and every other known species of the animal kingdom that have shown, by their behavior on earth, they deserve to be here. You play with any one you want or none at all-it's up to you. The angels pet you and praise you when you have been especially good and they will even play with you, if you want. It's Heaven.

There is one main Palace and then many homes scattered over the clouds. Everybody sleeps on the white fluffy clouds, using them as beds; even the pets do. They are extremely comfortable and cooler than the marble slabs were in our Highland Park home.

I do miss Puddin and Bobby. I can look down and check on them whenever I want. I can tell what they are doing at all times. I wonder if they miss me too. I miss the big house in Highland Park. I miss my friend Janice, but most of all I miss my special Puddin.

After I got to Heaven I looked down and saw Bobby digging a hole in the side yard. He gently placed a little white bundle, about my size, into the hole. He then positioned a stone at the head of the hole after he covered the cloth wrapped bundle with dirt. I could even see what he wrote on the stone. It read "Tiff, 1983-1999-The Best."

I saw the epitaph and I couldn't stop crying. I could also see by the movement of his shoulders and head that he was crying too. I knew Puddin originally gave me to him as a Valentine's gift but I didn't realize he cared for me that much. A sense of poignancy overwhelmed me like I had never experienced before. I often reflect on that scene. It constantly reminds me of the enormous love and devotion heaped on me by human parents and how lucky I am that Puddin chose me from all the other puppies in the kennel. I *am* blessed.

I'm getting to know my way around up here. St. Peter tells me if I work hard and continue to be a good dog I will get my wings. That means I can be guardian angel for an earthling pet. I can come and go as I like, if it is on a mission. I haven't tried it but I understand guardian angels can take pets down to earth so they can check on their previous life. I think I will wait until I get my own wings rather than depend on someone else.

St. Peter even talked about moving me over to the Palace since I am a Lhasa Apso, but then the Palace doesn't need guarding since there are no threats in Heaven. I'll do whatever they want, I am just glad to be here as opposed to the "Other Place."

I remembered my human parents talking about my personality and how moody I could be. Bobby even said it was almost as though I was letting them live with me. They loved me because I was not one of those gushy, slobbering, and overfriendly lap dogs. True, I barked a lot, but I was supposed to do that; The Tibetan Monks bred that trait into our breed. I was very discriminating. I was the ultimate lady and still am. I was finicky, fastidious, and sensitive. That is saying a lot about a dog-I know. Sometimes I wonder how I got up here, but that's me-I can't help it.

I don't wish anything bad for Puddin and Bobby, but I do hope they will hurry and get up here. I'll let them live with me again, forever, in Heaven.

THE END

Printed in the United States
By Bookmasters